Jesus:
Experiencing
His Touch

Kay Arthur & David Arthur

PRECEPT MINISTRIES INTERNATIONAL

WATERBROOK
PRESS

JESUS: EXPERIENCING HIS TOUCH

Trade Paperback ISBN 978-1-60142-806-6
eBook ISBN 978-1-60142-807-3

Cover design by The Designworks Group

Published in the United States by WaterBrook, an imprint of the Crown Publishing Group, a division of Penguin Random House LLC, New York.

WATERBROOK® and its deer colophon are registered trademarks of Penguin Random House LLC.

Printed in the United States of America
2018

10 9 8 7 6 5

SPECIAL SALES
Most WaterBrook books are available at special quantity discounts when purchased in bulk by corporations, organizations, and special-interest groups. Custom imprinting or excerpting can also be done to fit special needs. For information, please e-mail specialmarketscms @penguinrandomhouse.com or call 1-800-603-7051.

CONTENTS

This small-group study is for people who are interested in learning for themselves more about what the Bible says on various subjects, but who have only limited time to meet together. It's ideal, for example, for a lunch group at work, an early morning men's group, a young mothers' group meeting in a home, a Sunday-school class, or even family devotions. (It's also ideal for small groups that typically have longer meeting times—such as evening groups or Saturday morning groups—but want to devote only a portion of their time together to actual study, while reserving the rest for prayer, fellowship, or other activities.)

This book is designed so that all the group's participants will complete each lesson's study activities *at the same time.* Discussing your insights drawn from what God says about the subject reveals exciting, life-impacting truths.

Although it's a group study, you'll need a facilitator to lead the study and keep the discussion moving. If *you* are your group's facilitator, the leader, here are some helpful points for making your job easier:

- Go through the lesson and mark the text before you lead the group. This will give you increased familiarity with the material and will enable you to facilitate the group with greater ease. It may be easier for you to lead the group through the instructions for marking if you, as a leader, choose a specific color for each symbol you mark.

- As you lead the group, start at the beginning of the text and simply read it aloud in the order it appears in the lesson, including the Insight boxes that appear throughout. Work through the lesson together, observing and discussing what you learn. As you read the Scripture verses, have the group say aloud the word they are marking in the text.

- The discussion questions are there simply to help you cover the material. As the class moves into the discussion, many times you will find that they will cover the questions on their own. Remember, the discussion questions are there to guide the group through the topic, not to squelch discussion.

- Remember how important it is for people to verbalize their answers and discoveries. This greatly strengthens their personal understanding of each week's lesson. Try to ensure that everyone has plenty of opportunity to contribute to each week's discussions.

- Keep the discussion moving. This may mean spending more time on some parts of the study than on others. If necessary, you should feel free to spread out a lesson over more than one session. However, remember that you don't want to slow the pace too much. It's much better to leave everyone wanting more than to have people dropping out because of declining interest.

- If the validity or accuracy of some of the answers seems questionable, you can gently and cheerfully remind the group to stay focused on the truth of the Scriptures. Your object is to learn what the Bible says, not to engage in human philosophy. Simply stick with the Scriptures and give God the opportunity to speak. His Word *is* truth (John 17:17)!

JESUS: EXPERIENCING HIS TOUCH

People hold all sorts of opinions about Jesus Christ—what He believed, what He taught, how He lived. They also have thoughts on how He died and whether or not He really rose from the dead. But when you set opinions aside, what do you know for yourself about Jesus? What does Jesus mean to you? How have you encountered Him firsthand?

The Bible is unlike any other book ever written. It offers us sixty-six books written by God through the agency of man. The words found in the Scriptures bring spirit and life to us because they are God-breathed and inspired by the Spirit of God. Jesus Himself told us in Matthew 4:4 that man is to live by "every word that proceeds out of the mouth of God." This means we can encounter Christ each day by engaging with the Word of God—and that in doing so we will find our very lives transformed.

During the next six weeks we'll be reading and discussing the first six chapters in the gospel of Mark, looking at what happened to those who encountered Jesus firsthand. You're going to see how lives were transformed by the presence and touch of the Savior. And you'll experience for yourself the difference it makes when you engage with Jesus personally and experience His touch in your life.

Life is not easy for anyone, but when you know Jesus for yourself—when you understand His character, His proclamations, His teaching, His power, His authority, and what it means to be His follower—that knowledge becomes a steppingstone to living life with certainty and confidence. And that assurance is strengthened with every decision to live according to the truths of God's Word.

OBSERVE

Leader: *Read Mark 1:1–3 aloud with the group. Then read it aloud a second time. Read slowly and have the group say aloud and mark each key word as directed:*

- *Mark every reference to **Jesus Christ** with a cross:* †*. In the same way, mark any synonyms, such as **Son of God** and **Lord**, as well as any pronouns, such as **you**, that refer to Jesus Christ. Since you'll be marking references to Jesus so often, you may prefer to use a particular color to mark the references to Him so they pop on the page.*
- *Draw a squiggly line under the word **messenger**, like this:* ∿∿ *Include pronouns such as **who** and synonyms such as **voice**.*

MARK 1:1–3

1 The beginning of the gospel of Jesus Christ, the Son of God.

2 As it is written in Isaiah the prophet: "Behold, I send My messenger ahead of You, who will prepare Your way;

3 The voice of one crying in the wilderness, 'Make ready the way of the Lord, make His paths straight.'"

As you read the text, it's helpful to have the group say the key words aloud as they mark them. This way everyone will be sure they are marking every occurrence of the word, including any synonymous words or phrases. Do this throughout the study.

INSIGHT

The word *gospel* means good news.

Christ is the Greek word for Messiah. The Messiah was the anointed One whose coming was prophesied in the Old Testament.

DISCUSS

• Starting at verse 1 and moving through verse 3, look at every place where you marked a reference to Jesus Christ and state what you learned about Him from marking the text.

• Now discuss what you learn about the messenger from Isaiah's prophecy.

OBSERVE

Leader: *Read Mark 1:4–8 aloud, slowly. Have the group do the following:*

- *Draw a squiggly line like water* ∼∼∼ *under all references to John the Baptist, including pronouns such as him and he.*
- *Mark all references to baptism with a squiggly line both above and underneath the word, like this:* ∼∼∼
- *Mark each occurrence of the word sins with a big S.*
- *Mark all references to the Spirit of God like this:* ◠◠

DISCUSS

- Look at the places where you marked references to John. What does the text tell you about him? What was he called, where was he, and what was he doing?

MARK 1:4–8

4 John the Baptist appeared in the wilderness preaching a baptism of repentance for the forgiveness of sins.

5 And all the country of Judea was going out to him, and all the people of Jerusalem; and they were being baptized by him in the Jordan River, confessing their sins.

6 John was clothed with camel's hair and wore a leather belt around his waist, and his diet was locusts and wild honey.

7 And he was preaching, and saying, "After me One is coming who is mightier than I, and I am not

fit to stoop down and untie the thong of His sandals.

8 "I baptized you with water; but He will baptize you with the Holy Spirit."

INSIGHT

The verb *baptize* is the simple transliteration of the Greek verb *baptizo*. In the Koine (common) Greek, it was used in reference to dyeing cloth and making pickles. The cloth takes on the color of the dye, and the cucumber absorbs the flavor of the brine. Thus baptism symbolizes unification, identification with Christ.

• What kind of a baptism was John preaching in verse 4? What purpose did it serve?

• Describe the response of the people to John's message.

INSIGHT

To *repent* is to change one's mind on something, which consequently leads to a change of belief and/or a change of behavior.

• Who do you think John was talking about in verses 7 and 8? Explain your answer.

• According to verse 8, what would that person do?

OBSERVE

Leader: Read Mark 1:9–13 aloud. Have the group do the following:
- *Mark all references to **Jesus**, including pronouns and synonyms, with a cross or with the color they chose.*
- *Double underline anything that tells you **where** something takes place, for instance, **Nazareth in Galilee**, **the Jordan**, or **the wilderness**.*
- *Place a check mark like this ✓ over the word **immediately**.*
- *Mark references to **the Spirit** like this:*

- *Mark **Satan** with a pitchfork, like this:*

MARK 1:9–13

9 In those days Jesus came from Nazareth in Galilee and was baptized by John in the Jordan.

10 Immediately coming up out of the water, He saw the heavens opening, and the Spirit like a dove descending upon Him;

11 and a voice came out of the heavens: "You are My beloved Son, in You I am well-pleased."

12 Immediately the Spirit impelled Him to go out into the wilderness.

13 And He was in the wilderness forty days being tempted by Satan; and He was with the wild beasts, and the angels were ministering to Him.

DISCUSS

• What do you learn from marking the references to Jesus in verses 9–11? Where was He? What happened?

• Who is speaking in verse 11, and what do you learn from Him about Jesus?

• What happened to Jesus in verses 12 and 13?

• What do you learn from marking *the Spirit*?

MARK 1:14–20

14 Now after John had been taken into custody, Jesus came into Galilee, preaching the gospel of God,

15 and saying, "The time is fulfilled, and the kingdom of God is at hand;

OBSERVE

Leader: Read Mark 1:14–20 aloud. Have the group do the following:

• *Draw a squiggly line under each reference to John.*

• *Mark each reference to Jesus as they did previously.*

• *Put a check mark over the word immediately.*

• *Mark follow and followed like this:*

DISCUSS

• What does Mark tell you about John the Baptist in the beginning of this passage?

• According to verses 14–15, where did Jesus go, what did He do, and when did He do it?

• Look at verses 16–20. Where was Jesus, who did He come into contact with, and what did He call them to do?

repent and believe in the gospel."

16 As He was going along by the Sea of Galilee, He saw Simon and Andrew, the brother of Simon, casting a net in the sea; for they were fishermen.

17 And Jesus said to them, "Follow Me, and I will make you become fishers of men."

18 Immediately they left their nets and followed Him.

19 Going on a little farther, He saw James the son of Zebedee, and John his brother, who were also in the boat mending the nets.

20 Immediately He called them; and they

left their father
Zebedee in the boat
with the hired ser-
vants, and went away
to follow Him.

• How did they respond?

• What do you think Jesus meant when He said, "I will make you become fishers of men"?

MARK 1:21–28

21 They went into
Capernaum; and
immediately on the
Sabbath He entered
the synagogue and
began to teach.

22 They were amazed
at His teaching; for
He was teaching them
as one having author-

OBSERVE

Leader: Read Mark 1:21–28 aloud and slowly. Have the group do the following:

*• Mark each reference to **Jesus** as they have previously.*

*• Double underline anything that indicates **where Jesus was.***

*• Put a check mark over the word **immediately**.*

*• Mark all references to **unclean spirits,** including pronouns, with a pitchfork, ψ, since they are part of Satan's team.*

DISCUSS

• Where was Jesus in verses 21–22, and what was He doing?

• Look at the map below to identify the location of the city and synagogue mentioned in these verses.

Israel in the Time of Christ

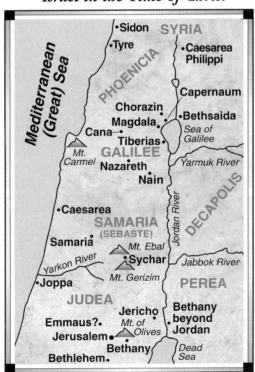

ity, and not as the scribes.

23 Just then there was a man in their synagogue with an unclean spirit; and he cried out,

24 saying, "What business do we have with each other, Jesus of Nazareth? Have You come to destroy us? I know who You are—the Holy One of God!"

25 And Jesus rebuked him, saying, "Be quiet, and come out of him!"

26 Throwing him into convulsions, the unclean spirit cried out with a loud voice and came out of him.

27 They were all amazed, so that they

debated among them-
selves, saying, "What
is this? A new teaching
with authority! He
commands even the
unclean spirits, and
they obey Him."

28 Immediately the
news about Him
spread everywhere into
all the surrounding
district of Galilee.

• What was the response of those around Jesus?

• What happened next, and how did Jesus handle it, according to verses 23–25?

• Look at all those pitchforks! Move through the text and discuss what you learn about this unclean spirit.

INSIGHT

Synagogues were the official meeting place for the Jewish people in New Testament times. They became centers of learning and worship where the people gathered to read from the Law and the Prophets, pray, and hear messages from those invited to speak.

Synagogues came into being after the Jews were sent into exile under the Babylonians. Separated from Jerusalem and their temple, exiles established synagogues as a means of preserving their faith. They first sprang up outside the land of Israel and then were established throughout the land after the Jewish people returned from exile.

• What was the reaction of those who watched Jesus interact with the unclean spirit?

• If you have time, discuss what impressed you the most as you observed these first 28 verses of the first chapter of Mark.

WRAP IT UP

Three times in our text this week we saw the word *gospel.* Verse 1 speaks of the beginning of the gospel of Jesus Christ. Verses 14 and 15 speak of Jesus proclaiming the gospel of God.

The gospel is literally "the good news." But what good news? Often we think of the gospel as the collected facts about Jesus' death, burial, and resurrection. This definition is accurate and spelled out clearly in places like 1 Corinthians 15. But what is the gospel, the good news in Mark 1? Jesus had not yet died on the cross; in fact, He had just begun His ministry.

Verse 15 tells us more of the good news Jesus preached: "The time is fulfilled, and the kingdom of God is at hand."

Something long awaited for—something amazing and powerful— is at hand: the kingdom of God! So what are we to do? How are we to respond?

Jesus says in verse 15, "Repent and believe in the gospel." What does it mean to repent and believe? Without taking away the joy of discovering all that is coming our way in this study, let's start with what happened next. Jesus said to the fishermen, "Follow Me."

As we study the gospel of Mark together, let's be intentional about following Jesus. Let's focus our minds and hearts on what it means to believe in the gospel, to repent and follow Jesus, to draw near and experience His touch on our lives.

Last week we covered the first 28 verses of Mark. Did you notice how succinctly the gospel writer covers his material? "Immediately" is not only a key repeated word; it's indicative of the pace at which Mark tells the story. No wonder it is the shortest of all the Gospels!

Matthew, Luke, and John fill in the details and elaborate on Jesus' teachings. However, Mark wrote during a time of crisis under the reign of Nero, when Christians were being arrested, tortured, and put to death. It is within this context that Mark tells us about the good news, "the gospel of Jesus Christ, the Son of God" (1:1) and quickly moves on to what we need to know next.

Before we move on, let's take a minute to review what we've covered and ensure we fully grasp the context of the scenes we're about to encounter.

So far we've met John the Baptist, the one prophesied by Isaiah who would prepare the way for Jesus and the forgiveness of sins. Forgiveness of sins is good news, the promise for all who believe in Jesus.

After Jesus' baptism, like the finger of God, the Spirit descended on Jesus and God spoke from heaven, declaring He was pleased with His Son. Then Jesus went into the wilderness to be tempted by Satan.

John was taken into custody. Jesus, moving along the shores of the Sea of Galilee, called fishermen to follow Him and become fishers of men. Immediately they went fishing in a synagogue! As Jesus taught, the people were amazed at His authority.

When an unclean spirit took the floor, Jesus commanded it to leave. And leave it did, in the drama of a convulsion! Immediately the news of Jesus' authority over the forces of the Evil One spread into the surrounding district of Galilee.

MARK 1:29–34

29 And immediately after they came out of the synagogue, they came into the house of Simon and Andrew, with James and John.

30 Now Simon's mother-in-law was lying sick with a fever; and immediately they spoke to Jesus about her.

31 And He came to her and raised her up, taking her by the hand, and the fever left her, and she waited on them.

32 When evening came, after the sun had set, they began bringing to Him all who were ill and those who were demon-possessed.

33 And the whole city had gathered at the door.

OBSERVE

Let's pick up where we left off, after Jesus cast out an unclean spirit in the synagogue in Capernaum.

Leader: Read Mark 1:29–34 aloud. Have the group do the following:

- *Mark every reference to **Jesus,** including pronouns, with a cross or with the color they've chosen.*
- *Double underline anything that tells **where Jesus was** geographically, any reference to a city, an area, or a district.*
- *Mark each reference to **demons** with a pitchfork: ⚆*
- *Mark every reference to **illness** with a downward semicircle, like this: ⌒*

DISCUSS

- What happened in verses 29–31 after Jesus and His disciples came out of the synagogue?

- What do you learn in these verses about Simon (later called Peter) and his mother-in-law?

• In verse 32, what happened after the sun had set?

• Drawing on what you read last week, why had such a crowd gathered in verse 33?

34 And He healed many who were ill with various diseases, and cast out many demons; and He was not permitting the demons to speak, because they knew who He was.

OBSERVE

Leader: Read Mark 1:35–45 aloud. Have the group say aloud and mark the key words as follows:

• *Mark each reference to **Jesus** as they have previously.*
• *Circle references to* time.
• *Double underline every indication of* **geographical location.**
• *Draw a pitchfork over any reference to* **demons.**
• *Mark each mention of **the leper** and **leprosy**, including pronouns, as you marked* illness, *like this:*

Mark 1:35–45

35 In the early morning, while it was still dark, Jesus got up, left the house, and went away to a secluded place, and was praying there.

36 Simon and his companions searched for Him;

37 they found Him, and said to Him, "Everyone is looking for You."

38 He said to them, "Let us go somewhere else to the towns nearby, so that I may preach there also; for that is what I came for."

39 And He went into their synagogues throughout all Galilee, preaching and casting out the demons.

40 And a leper came to Jesus, beseeching Him and falling on his knees before Him, and saying, "If You are willing, You can make me clean."

41 Moved with compassion, Jesus stretched out His hand and touched him, and said to him, "I am willing; be cleansed."

DISCUSS

• How did Jesus begin His day? Get the details!

• What, if anything, might we learn from His example?

• What do you learn from marking the references to the leper?

INSIGHT

According to Leviticus 13:3, *leprosy* was an infectious skin disease with specific symptoms—whitened hair and pustular sores "deeper than the skin." On contact the disease could spread to other persons and even to inanimate objects like clothes and houses (Leviticus 14:33–57).

When a priest's prognosis was positive, he declared the victim "unclean." As long as he had the disease, the victim had to "live alone...outside the camp" (Leviticus 13:46–47). Healing and restoration required atonement by several offerings (Leviticus 14:10–20).

• How did Jesus deal with the leper? Why is this significant? How does Jesus' response compare with how lepers were commonly treated at the time?

• What does Jesus' example suggest about how we as His followers should respond to the outcasts, the vulnerable, the rejects of society?

42 Immediately the leprosy left him and he was cleansed.

43 And He sternly warned him and immediately sent him away,

44 and He said to him, "See that you say nothing to anyone; but go, show yourself to the priest and offer for your cleansing what Moses commanded, as a testimony to them."

45 But he went out and began to proclaim it freely and to spread the news around, to such an extent that Jesus could no longer publicly enter a city, but stayed out in unpopulated areas; and they were coming to Him from everywhere.

MARK 2:1–12

¹ When He had come back to Capernaum several days afterward, it was heard that He was at home.

² And many were gathered together, so that there was no longer room, not even near the door; and He was speaking the word to them.

³ And they came, bringing to Him a paralytic, carried by four men.

⁴ Being unable to get to Him because of the crowd, they removed the roof above Him; and when they had dug an opening, they let down the pallet on which the paralytic was lying.

OBSERVE

Now that we've carefully marked and studied Mark 1, our goal is to move through Mark 2 incident by incident while looking for any recurring themes.

Leader: Read Mark 2:1–12 aloud. Have the group mark…

- ***Jesus,*** *including pronouns and the phrase* **Son of Man,** *as before.*
- *each mention of the* **paralytic** *as you marked* illness, *with a downward semicircle.*
- **sins** *with a big* **S.** *If* **forgiveness** *is mentioned in connection with sin, then put a slash through the* **S.**
- *each reference to* **the scribes,** *including pronouns, with a big* **P.** *(We will later mark* Pharisees *the same way, as the two groups are often associated together.)*

INSIGHT

Pharisee means "separated one." This term likely was used to describe these men because they separated themselves from the strong influence of the classical Greek culture of Hellenism. Hellenism arose in the intertestamental period (the years between the writing of the Old and New Testaments), a time when many Jews took on Greek ways.

During New Testament times, the majority of the scribes were Pharisees whose mission was to teach the Law of God. Scribes were skilled writers, often trained in the Word of God and thus considered experts in the Law and interpreting it.

DISCUSS

• Where was Jesus and what was He doing before the paralytic was lowered into the room?

5 And Jesus seeing their faith said to the paralytic, "Son, your sins are forgiven."

6 But some of the scribes were sitting there and reasoning in their hearts,

7 "Why does this man speak that way? He is blaspheming; who can forgive sins but God alone?"

8 Immediately Jesus, aware in His spirit that they were reasoning that way within themselves, said to them, "Why are you reasoning about these things in your hearts?

9 "Which is easier, to say to the paralytic, 'Your sins are forgiven'; or to say, 'Get

up, and pick up your pallet and walk'?

10 "But so that you may know that the Son of Man has authority on earth to forgive sins"—He said to the paralytic,

11 "I say to you, get up, pick up your pallet and go home."

12 And he got up and immediately picked up the pallet and went out in the sight of everyone, so that they were all amazed and were glorifying God, saying, "We have never seen anything like this."

• What do you learn about the paralytic and the way Jesus dealt with him?

• What do you learn about the scribes? How did Jesus deal with them?

• What do you learn from marking the references to sin in these verses?

• How did Jesus refer to Himself in verse 10, and what does that tell you about Him?

• So where is the first place we are to go when we sin?

INSIGHT

The term *Son of Man* appears in the Old and New Testaments. In the Old Testament it is used to stress the humanity of a person, for example Ezekiel the prophet. However, in Daniel 7 the term is used in connection with Messiah receiving a kingdom bestowed upon Him by God Himself, the Ancient of Days.

In respect to Jesus, the title *Son of Man* emphasizes His humanity without discounting His deity. Jesus was God in the flesh.

MARK 2:13–17

13 And He went out again by the seashore; and all the people were coming to Him, and He was teaching them.

14 As He passed by, He saw Levi the son of Alphaeus sitting in the tax booth, and He said to him, "Follow Me!" And he got up and followed Him.

15 And it happened that He was reclining at the table in his house, and many tax collectors and sinners were dining with Jesus and His disciples; for there were many of them, and they were following Him.

16 When the scribes of the Pharisees saw

OBSERVE

Leader: Read Mark 2:13–17 aloud. Have *the group do the following:*

• *Mark each reference to* **Jesus** *as before.*
• *Mark* **scribes** *with a big* **P.**
• *Draw an arrow under* **follow, followed,** *and* **following,** *like this:* ——>
• *Mark* **sinners** *with a big* **S.**

INSIGHT

Tax collectors were members of a political office created to collect taxes in the provinces under Rome. They often collected an additional portion for themselves. Obviously they were not liked by the populace.

DISCUSS

• What was Jesus doing in this passage, and who did He encounter?

• Describe the interaction between Jesus and Levi. Where did Jesus encounter Levi, and how did Levi respond to Jesus' invitation?

• What do you learn from marking *sinners*?

• What caused the scribes to question Jesus' actions, and how did Jesus respond?

• What lesson can you learn from Jesus' actions in this passage?

that He was eating with the sinners and tax collectors, they said to His disciples, "Why is He eating and drinking with tax collectors and sinners?"

17 And hearing this, Jesus said to them, "It is not those who are healthy who need a physician, but those who are sick; I did not come to call the righteous, but sinners."

MARK 2:18–22

18 John's disciples and the Pharisees were fasting; and they came and said to Him, "Why do John's disciples and the disciples of the Pharisees fast, but Your disciples do not fast?"

19 And Jesus said to them, "While the bridegroom is with them, the attendants of the bridegroom cannot fast, can they? So long as they have the bridegroom with them, they cannot fast.

20 "But the days will come when the bridegroom is taken away from them, and then they will fast in that day.

OBSERVE

Leader: *Read Mark 2:18–22 aloud. Have the group…*

- *mark* **Jesus** *and* **bridegroom** *the same way.*
- *circle* **fasting** *and draw a slash through it, like this:* ⊘
- *mark each mention of the* **Pharisees** *with a big* **P.**
- *draw an arrow under* **disciples,** *like this:* ⟶

Leader: *Since this is not an easy passage to grasp, read it aloud again.*

INSIGHT

To *fast* is to do without—without food and sometimes without water. In biblical times, fasting was viewed as an act of piety, a way to draw near to God. Jesus was fasting when He was tempted by the devil in the wilderness. Acts 9:9 describes a time when Paul went without food and water. The Pharisees routinely fasted two times a week.

Wineskins were made from goat-skins, which were soft and pliable and able to expand to hold the gases produced by the fermenting wine. Old wineskins could not handle new wine because they lost their flexibility.

21 "No one sews a patch of unshrunk cloth on an old garment; otherwise the patch pulls away from it, the new from the old, and a worse tear results.

22 "No one puts new wine into old wine-skins; otherwise the wine will burst the skins, and the wine is lost and the skins as well; but one puts new wine into fresh wine-skins."

DISCUSS

• What behavior is questioned here? Which groups of people were being contrasted?

• How did Jesus respond to the controversy?

• What analogy did Jesus use, and what does it reveal about Jesus?

• What two illustrations did Jesus use in verses 21 and 22? What was His point? Reread Mark 1:7–8, 14–15.

MARK 2:23–28

23 And it happened that He was passing through the grain-fields on the Sabbath, and His disciples began to make their way along while picking the heads of grain.

24 The Pharisees were saying to Him, "Look, why are they doing what is not lawful on the Sabbath?"

25 And He said to them, "Have you never read what David did when he was in need and he and his companions became hungry;

26 how he entered the house of God in the time of Abiathar the high priest, and ate the

OBSERVE

Leader: *Read Mark 2:23–28 aloud. Have the group mark…*

- *each reference to **Jesus,** including **Son of Man,** as before.*
- *each occurrence of the word **Sabbath** with a big 7.*
- *every mention of **the disciples** with an arrow.*
- ***Pharisees** with a big **P.***

INSIGHT

The word *Sabbath* comes from the Hebrew verb *Shabbat,* which means "to stop." The Sabbath observance marked the day God rested following six days of creating the universe (Genesis 2:1–2). In Exodus 20:8, 11, as one of the Ten Commandments, God instructed His people to "remember the sabbath day, to keep it holy" and told them not to work on the seventh day.

DISCUSS

• What is the issue in these verses, and who raised it?

• How did Jesus answer the concern?

• What was Jesus' bottom line in regard to the Sabbath? How might this perspective benefit us today?

consecrated bread, which is not lawful for anyone to eat except the priests, and he also gave it to those who were with him?"

27 Jesus said to them, "The Sabbath was made for man, and not man for the Sabbath.

28 "So the Son of Man is Lord even of the Sabbath."

WRAP IT UP

Simon Peter's mother-in-law and the leper both were healed in their encounter with Jesus—at just a touch from Him. And it was immediate!

To touch a leper in those days was not only forbidden, it was repulsive. Yet Jesus, demonstrating His love coupled with His power and authority, touched and healed the outcasts. Can you imagine what it must have been like to be touched by Jesus and to be set free? To be completely healed?

Wouldn't that be awesome?

Yet, did you notice the scene wedged into our text that gives us a glimpse of the source and purpose of Christ's mission? Before the sun rose, Jesus went to talk with His Father in private. In the fifth chapter of the gospel of John, we read that Jesus Himself said He never acted independently of the Father. His works and words are the Father's! His mission is God's. In Mark 1:35–39 He declared that He came to preach, to proclaim the good news of who He is.

The healings and the casting out of demons who served the devil himself simply demonstrated that Jesus was the Son of Man, the Son of God—and unless people believed that reality they would perish. As He said, "That is what I came for" (Mark 1:38). How about you? What is your purpose? Are you ready, if He asks you to do so, to leave it all like the fishermen and tax collector and respond to Christ's call to "follow Me"?

If so, beloved of God, He'll direct your steps and He will touch the lives of others through yours as you seek to do the will of your Father in heaven.

Have you ever had to deal with a clique of jealous people who viewed you as competition? Or maybe an individual or group didn't like you or what you stood for? A group whose values or perspective on life was so different that they made it clear to all around that you weren't one of them—and for that reason they wanted you out of the way?

If so, you aren't alone.

OBSERVE

Leader: *Read Mark 3:1–6 aloud. Have the group...*

- *mark the references to **Jesus** with a cross or color, as before.*
- *mark any reference to **the Pharisees**, including pronouns, with a big **P**.*
- *mark each occurrence of the word **Sabbath** with a big **7**.*

DISCUSS

- What was going on in the synagogue?

- What did Jesus do? How did He handle this situation?

MARK 3:1–6

1 He entered again into a synagogue; and a man was there whose hand was withered.

2 They were watching Him to see if He would heal him on the Sabbath, so that they might accuse Him.

3 He said to the man with the withered hand, "Get up and come forward!"

4 And He said to them, "Is it lawful to do good or to do harm

on the Sabbath, to save a life or to kill?" But they kept silent.

5 After looking around at them with anger, grieved at their hardness of heart, He said to the man, "Stretch out your hand." And he stretched it out, and his hand was restored.

6 The Pharisees went out and immediately began conspiring with the Herodians against Him, as to how they might destroy Him.

• How did Jesus feel toward the Pharisees, and why?

• What insight does this give you? Is all anger wrong?

INSIGHT

The Herodians were an elite aristocratic Galilean-based group that favored the policies of Herod Antipas, politically siding with the Roman government. Herod Antipas was tetrarch of Galilee (Luke 3:1).

• What did you learn about the Pharisees and the Herodians in regard to Jesus?

OBSERVE

Leader: Read Mark 3:7–12 aloud. Have the group do the following:

- *Mark every reference to **Jesus**.*
- *Double underline anything that indicates **where**.*
- *Draw an arrow under each reference to **the disciples**.*
- *Mark references to **unclean spirits** and **demons** with a pitchfork.*

DISCUSS

- According to verses 7–8 and the map on the following page, what do you learn about Jesus and those who came to Him?

MARK 3:7–12

7 Jesus withdrew to the sea with His disciples; and a great multitude from Galilee followed; and also from Judea,

8 and from Jerusalem, and from Idumea, and beyond the Jordan, and the vicinity of Tyre and Sidon, a great number of people heard of all that He was doing and came to Him.

9 And He told His disciples that a boat should stand ready for Him because of the crowd, so that they would not crowd Him;

10 for He had healed many, with the result

that all those who had afflictions pressed around Him in order to touch Him.

11 Whenever the unclean spirits saw Him, they would fall down before Him and shout, "You are the Son of God!"

12 And He earnestly warned them not to tell who He was.

Israel in the Time of Christ

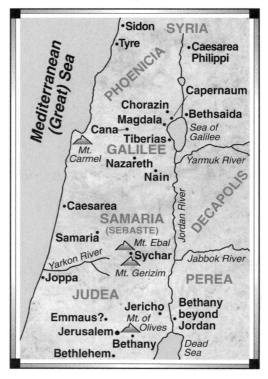

• What did the people want to do, and why? What was the purpose of the boat, and what does it tell you about what life was like for Jesus?

• What do you learn from marking the references to the unclean spirits?

OBSERVE

Leader: Read Mark 3:13–19 aloud. Have the group…

- *mark each reference to **Jesus** as before.*
- *double underline anything that indicates **where**.*
- *put a big **12** over references to **the twelve disciples**, including pronouns.*

DISCUSS

- What do you learn from marking references to the Twelve, apart from their names?

- List the names of the Twelve and anything the text tells you about each one.
  1.
  2.
  3.
  4.
  5.
  6.
  7.
  8.
  9.

MARK 3:13–19

13 And He went up on the mountain and summoned those whom He Himself wanted, and they came to Him.

14 And He appointed twelve, so that they would be with Him and that He could send them out to preach,

15 and to have authority to cast out the demons.

16 And He appointed the twelve: Simon (to whom He gave the name Peter),

17 and James, the son of Zebedee, and John the brother of James (to them He gave the name Boanerges,

which means, "Sons of Thunder");

18 and Andrew, and Philip, and Bartholomew, and Matthew, and Thomas, and James the son of Alphaeus, and Thaddaeus, and Simon the Zealot;

19 and Judas Iscariot, who betrayed Him.

10.

11.

12.

• What does Mark reveal about Judas right from the start? How could that information help the reader?

MARK 3:20–30

20 And He came home, and the crowd gathered again, to such an extent that they could not even eat a meal.

21 When His own people heard of this, they went out to take custody of Him; for they were saying, "He has lost His senses."

OBSERVE

Let's see what happened after Jesus appointed the Twelve to be with Him.

Leader: Read Mark 3:20–30 aloud and slowly. Have the group do the following:
- *Mark every reference to **Jesus.***
- *Mark **scribes** with a big **P**.*
- *Put a pitchfork over all references to **Beelzebul, demons,** and **Satan.***
- *Put a big **S** over **sin**.*

DISCUSS

• Where was Jesus, who was with Him, and what were the circumstances?

• Where did the scribes come from, and what accusations did they bring against Jesus in verse 22?

22 The scribes who came down from Jerusalem were saying, "He is possessed by Beelzebul," and "He casts out the demons by the ruler of the demons."

23 And He called them to Himself and began speaking to them in parables, "How can Satan cast out Satan?

24 "If a kingdom is divided against itself, that kingdom cannot stand.

25 "If a house is divided against itself, that house will not be able to stand.

26 "If Satan has risen up against himself and is divided, he cannot

stand, but he is fin-
ished!

27 "But no one can
enter the strong man's
house and plunder his
property unless he first
binds the strong man,
and then he will plun-
der his house.

28 "Truly I say to
you, all sins shall be
forgiven the sons of
men, and whatever
blasphemies they utter;

29 but whoever blas-
phemes against the
Holy Spirit never has
forgiveness, but is
guilty of an eternal
sin"—

30 because they were
saying, "He has an
unclean spirit."

• How did Jesus answer their accusation?
What logic did He present?

• What do you learn from marking *sin*?

• Considering the context of verses 28–29,
according to what Jesus said in verses
29–30, nothing more, nothing less, how
would you explain blaspheming the Holy
Spirit?

OBSERVE

Leader: *Read Mark 3:31–35 aloud. Have the group...*

- *mark every reference to **Jesus**.*
- *mark with a big **F** any reference to **family members**, including **mother, sister, brother**.*

DISCUSS

- Review what you just observed. What was the situation? Who was present?

- Why do you think Mark (under the direction of the Spirit of God) included this incident in his gospel? What do we learn from Jesus' answer?

- What's your relationship to Jesus? How do you know?

MARK 3:31–35

31 Then His mother and His brothers arrived, and standing outside they sent word to Him and called Him.

32 A crowd was sitting around Him, and they said to Him, "Behold, Your mother and Your brothers are outside looking for You."

33 Answering them, He said, "Who are My mother and My brothers?"

34 Looking about at those who were sitting around Him, He said, "Behold My mother and My brothers!

35 "For whoever does the will of God, he is My brother and sister and mother."

WRAP IT UP

Jesus picked His team. They weren't the religiously correct—no Pharisees! They weren't the elite, the politically correct—no Herodians. They weren't those residing in the holy city of Jerusalem. Instead, He chose twelve Galilean men from lowly professions. They responded to Jesus' call, leaving all to follow Him. Some were brothers, fishermen. Two were known by reputation as the Sons of Thunder! Another, Levi, also called Matthew (Matthew 9:9; 10:3), was a tax collector despised by his own people. And the twelfth was Judas, whom Jesus knew would betray Him (John 6:64).

Twelve disciples, just as there were twelve tribes of Israel. Israel, formerly called Jacob, was the second son of Isaac and yet was chosen by God over his brother Esau to receive the blessing and to be the father of His chosen people. Interesting, isn't it, how God so often elevates the lowly?

How did Jesus select and equip His band of brothers? He summoned those He wanted (Mark 3:13) to be with, those He could send out to preach (3:14) and invade the Enemy's stronghold by giving them authority to cast out demons.

The disciples were twelve unlikely individuals, chosen to proclaim His saving message to the entire world! Are you surprised? Are you encouraged to realize God can and will use anyone He chooses to achieve His purposes?

And who does He choose? Listen to the words God breathed through the apostle Paul in 1 Corinthians: "Consider your calling, brethren, that there were not many wise according to the flesh, not many mighty, not many noble; but God has chosen the foolish things of the world to shame the wise, and…the weak things…to shame the things which are strong, and the base things…and the despised God has chosen" (1:26–28).

And as we saw, the ones who are willing to do the will of God are those who qualify, the ones who comprise the real family of the Father and His Son, Jesus.

And so we leave you with this question: Do you qualify to be His brother, His sister, His mother? Have you responded to His touch, answered Jesus' summons to follow Him?

Jesus' ministry created a stir. The miracles and the teaching were new, unprecedented. No wonder crowds gathered around everywhere He went!

They witnessed what Jesus did, but did they truly see? Did they perceive what was happening? They heard what Jesus spoke, but did they get the message? And if they got the message, did they believe it?

And how about those of us who claim to follow Jesus today? Do we truly see and hear and understand?

Let's consider Jesus' picture of the kingdom of God as described through parables and see if we can grasp the truth He wanted His disciples to know.

OBSERVE

Leader: *Read Mark 4:1–9 aloud. Have the group say aloud and...*
- *mark each reference to **Jesus,** including pronouns, as they have previously.*
- *double underline anything that indicates a **location.** Watch carefully for references to where the seed falls.*
- *draw an oval around every mention of **seed(s),** including pronouns.*

MARK 4:1–9

1 He began to teach again by the sea. And such a very large crowd gathered to Him that He got into a boat in the sea and sat down; and the whole crowd was by the sea on the land.

2 And He was teaching them many things in parables, and was saying to them in His teaching,

3 "Listen to this! Behold, the sower went out to sow;

4 as he was sowing, some seed fell beside the road, and the birds came and ate it up.

5 "Other seed fell on the rocky ground where it did not have much soil; and immediately it sprang up because it had no depth of soil.

6 "And after the sun had risen, it was scorched; and because it had no root, it withered away.

7 "Other seed fell among the thorns, and the thorns came up and choked it, and it yielded no crop.

DISCUSS

• According to the first two verses of Mark 4, where was Jesus, what was He doing, and with whom? Answering these questions will give us the setting of this event.

• Where did the seed fall—in how many different places—and what happened to the seed in each place where it fell? Number the places as you discuss them.

• What was Jesus' exhortation to those present? What application, if any, do you see here for us as we study this gospel of Mark?

8 "Other seeds fell into the good soil, and as they grew up and increased, they yielded a crop and produced thirty, sixty, and a hundredfold."

9 And He was saying, "He who has ears to hear, let him hear."

OBSERVE

So what was the parable all about? Let's keep reading.

Leader: Read Mark 4:10–20 slowly and have the group do the following:

• Mark each reference to **Jesus.**

• Draw an arrow under every mention of the **followers** and the **twelve disciples** as a group, including pronouns such as **them** and **you** when they refer to the disciples.

• Mark **parable(s)** with a big question mark, like this: **?**

• Draw an oval around every reference to **word** and **seed.**

MARK 4:10–20

10 As soon as He was alone, His followers, along with the twelve, began asking Him about the parables.

11 And He was saying to them, "To you has been given the mystery of the kingdom of God, but those who are outside get everything in parables,

12 so that while seeing, they may see and

not perceive, and while hearing, they may hear and not understand, otherwise they might return and be forgiven."

13 And He said to them, "Do you not understand this parable? How will you understand all the parables?

14 "The sower sows the word.

15 "These are the ones who are beside the road where the word is sown; and when they hear, immediately Satan comes and takes away the word which has been sown in them.

16 "In a similar way these are the ones on whom seed was sown

DISCUSS

• What do you learn from marking *Jesus* and His *followers*?

• What do you learn about parables?

INSIGHT

A *parable* is a story that, although not usually factual, remains true to life and teaches a moral lesson or truth. Every detail of a parable will reinforce the main theme; however, you shouldn't always attempt to ascribe a specific spiritual meaning and application to each point.

Jesus frequently used parables in his teaching for two reasons: to reveal truth to believers and to hide truth from those who had rejected it and/or hardened their hearts against it.*

---

* Adapted from *The New Inductive Study Bible,* Precept Ministries International (Eugene, OR: Harvest House, 2013), 2104.

on the rocky places, who, when they hear the word, immediately receive it with joy;

17 and they have no firm root in themselves, but are only temporary; then, when affliction or persecution arises because of the word, immediately they fall away.

18 "And others are the ones on whom seed was sown among the thorns; these are the ones who have heard the word,

19 but the worries of the world, and the deceitfulness of riches, and the desires for other things enter in and choke the word, and it becomes unfruitful.

20 "And those are the ones on whom seed was sown on the good soil; and they hear the word and accept it and bear fruit, thirty, sixty, and a hundredfold."

OBSERVE

Leader: *Read the same text again. This time have the group do the following:*

- *Double underline __the places__ where the seed, the word, is sown.*
- *Mark references to **hear** with an ear, like this: ʔ*
- *Put a check mark over the word **immediately,** like this: ✓*
- *Mark **Satan** with a pitchfork: ↯*

DISCUSS

- What do you learn in verse 15 about the first place where the Word is sown? (Put a 1 at verse 15).

- How might this look? Maybe you've seen it happen; if so describe it.

- Read verses 16–17 and put a 2 next to verse 16. What do you learn about the second place where the Word is sown?

• What is the problem in this second place? Why the persecution, the affliction—and what happens as a result?

• Have you ever seen this scenario played out in real life? Without mentioning names, describe what happened.

• Read verses 18–19. Next to verse 18 put a 3. Discuss the three things that choke out the Word and what each of these might look like in a person's life today.

• Does this describe a fruitful or unfruitful life? Explain your answer.

• What can you learn from verses 18–19 that you can apply to your life? Do you find here a warning? A caution? Discuss your answer.

• Read verse 20 and mark it with a 4. What happens to the Word in this verse? Look at the three verbs. How does the response here compare with the other soils?

• And what makes it different from the other soils? Why is it described as it is?

• In these four examples given by Jesus, what's the variable—the seed or the soil—and what does this tell you?

• Look at where you marked *hear.* Which of the soils hear the Word and which bear fruit? What makes the difference in each case?

• What explanation would you give for the variance in the amount of fruit brought forth in the fourth scenario, and what does that say to you personally?

• So which of the soils would you say represents a genuine faith, and why?

• Which soil represents you?

OBSERVE

Leader: *Read Mark 4:21–34 aloud. Have the group…*

- *mark references to **Jesus** as they've been doing.*
- *put a symbol of an ear over the words **hear** and **listen:*** 𝒥
- *mark **word** with a book: 📖 Now that we've left the parable of the sower, use an open book like this to mark references to **the Word of God** and **the words of Jesus.***

Leader: *Read Mark 4:21–34 again so the group can better absorb what you are reading. This time have the group…*

- *draw a box around the phrase **the kingdom of God**.* ☐
- *mark the word **parable(s)** with a big question mark, like this:* **?**

DISCUSS

- What did Jesus tell His listeners in verses 21–25 that can serve as an exhortation or a caution for us?

MARK 4:21–34

21 And He was saying to them, "A lamp is not brought to be put under a basket, is it, or under a bed? Is it not brought to be put on the lampstand?

22 "For nothing is hidden, except to be revealed; nor has anything been secret, but that it would come to light.

23 "If anyone has ears to hear, let him hear."

24 And He was saying to them, "Take care what you listen to. By your standard of measure it will be measured to you; and more will be given you besides.

25 "For whoever has, to him more shall be given; and whoever

does not have, even what he has shall be taken away from him."

26 And He was saying, "The kingdom of God is like a man who casts seed upon the soil;

27 and he goes to bed at night and gets up by day, and the seed sprouts and grows—how, he himself does not know.

28 "The soil produces crops by itself; first the blade, then the head, then the mature grain in the head.

29 "But when the crop permits, he immediately puts in the sickle, because the harvest has come."

30 And He said, "How shall we picture the kingdom of God,

• What did you learn about the kingdom of God in verses 26–29?

• What did you learn from marking *kingdom* in verses 30–32?

• What new insights, if any, did you learn from marking *parable(s)* in this passage?

or by what parable shall we present it?

31 "It is like a mustard seed, which, when sown upon the soil, though it is smaller than all the seeds that are upon the soil,

32 yet when it is sown, it grows up and becomes larger than all the garden plants and forms large branches; so that the birds of the air can nest under its shade."

33 With many such parables He was speaking the word to them, so far as they were able to hear it;

34 and He did not speak to them without a parable; but He was explaining everything privately to His own disciples.

MARK 4:35–41

35 On that day, when evening came, He said to them, "Let us go over to the other side."

36 Leaving the crowd, they took Him along with them in the boat, just as He was; and other boats were with Him.

37 And there arose a fierce gale of wind, and the waves were breaking over the boat so much that the boat was already filling up.

38 Jesus Himself was in the stern, asleep on the cushion; and they woke Him and said to Him, "Teacher, do You not care that we are perishing?"

OBSERVE

As our study of this chapter comes to a close, the scene is about to change and the disciples are about to come to a new understanding.

Leader: Read Mark 4:35–41 aloud. Have the group do the following:
- *Mark each reference to Jesus.*
- *Mark the word them with an arrow, just as you've marked disciples.*
- *Draw a squiggly line under any reference to nature, such as wind, waves, sea.*

DISCUSS

- Describe the setting in verses 35–36. What is the situation, who is there, and where are they headed?

- What happened next?

• What was the disciples' attitude toward Jesus in verse 38, and why? Do you notice anything amiss in their thinking? If so, what?

• Now discuss the sequence of events in verses 38–40. You don't want to miss the order of what happens after they question Jesus' care of them.

• What do you think about the two questions Jesus asked the disciples? What do the questions reveal, and why is the timing important?

39 And He got up and rebuked the wind and said to the sea, "Hush, be still." And the wind died down and it became perfectly calm.

40 And He said to them, "Why are you afraid? Do you still have no faith?"

41 They became very much afraid and said to one another, "Who then is this, that even the wind and the sea obey Him?"

• How would faith have looked in this situation?

• What realization did the disciples come to, and how did it affect them, according to verse 41?

• What can you learn from this incident that can help you when you are afraid?

• What does this revelation of Jesus' power over nature suggest about His power over your life circumstances? How can that impact your perspective when trials come?

WRAP IT UP

"He who has ears to hear, let him hear." Twice Jesus makes this statement in our text. It's a signal that something very important is being said, so listen carefully! The message of the parable is made clear: not everyone will receive the Word of God.

Some have no interest in it at all; the Word is sown, Satan snatches it away, and they don't even know that it has come and gone. Others embrace it with joy and say they believe, but they don't put down roots into His Word; consequently, when trials and afflictions come, they can't handle the persecution that is ours if we are His! They fade away.

And then there are those who say they believe, who profess to be followers of Jesus Christ but don't have time for God. Rather than being overcomers, they are overcome by the worries of the world, the deceitfulness of riches, and the desire for things over God. The Word is choked right out of their daily lives and they bear no fruit.

How do we truly know we have heard? What is an indicator that we have ears to hear?

There's fruit in our lives! Jesus said it: the good soil hears God's Word, accepts it, and bears fruit. Some more than others—thus the thirty, the sixty, the hundredfold—but always there is a measure of fruit when God's Word takes root in our lives.

Mark only used the word *faith* five times in his entire gospel. We find it in verse 40 when Jesus asked His disciples, "Why are you afraid? Do you still have no faith?"

The disciples were in the boat with the One who not only created the earth but upholds it simply by the power of His Word (Hebrews 1:1–2). If they believed that, they had no reason to fear.

Having faith is having ears to hear. Having faith is having trust in Jesus to be and to do what He says.

So what is happening in your life, beloved of God, as you do this study? Are you accepting…believing…*living* the truth God has written and preserved for you in His Word?

When the storms come, just remember Jesus does care. Stop trembling, take your eyes off the storm, and fear—trust—Him alone.

And watch for the harvest that will come from the good soil of your heart!

Have you ever felt utterly abandoned and alone? Have you felt unloved…even unlovable?

In this week's study we'll learn more about how the Savior engaged with individuals who were alone in their circumstances—and how His touch and love transformed everything.

OBSERVE

Leader: *Read Mark 5:1–13 aloud. Read it slowly enough to absorb the hopelessness reflected in the opening verses. Have the group do the following:*

- *Double underline anything that tells you __where__ the action is taking place.*
- *Mark each reference to **Jesus,** beginning with the word **He** in verse 2.*
- *Draw a box around every reference to **the man with an unclean spirit** and mark it with a pitchfork.*
- *Mark all references to **the unclean spirit** and **demons** with a pitchfork.*

MARK 5:1–13

1 They came to the other side of the sea, into the country of the Gerasenes.

2 When He got out of the boat, immediately a man from the tombs with an unclean spirit met Him,

3 and he had his dwelling among the tombs. And no one was able to bind him anymore, even with a chain;

4 because he had often been bound with

shackles and chains, and the chains had been torn apart by him and the shackles broken in pieces, and no one was strong enough to subdue him.

5 Constantly, night and day, he was screaming among the tombs and in the mountains, and gashing himself with stones.

6 Seeing Jesus from a distance, he ran up and bowed down before Him;

7 and shouting with a loud voice, he said, "What business do we have with each other, Jesus, Son of the Most High God? I implore

DISCUSS

• Describe the situation of the man with an unclean spirit.

• How did this story hit you? Can you imagine being in that man's condition? As you think of his isolation, his pain, his hopelessness, how does it make you feel, and why?

• Look at the places you marked with a pitchfork. What do you learn about unclean spirits and demons?

• What did these demons know about Jesus, according to verse 7? What does that tell you about them and their relationship to Jesus?

You by God, do not torment me!"

8 For He had been saying to him, "Come out of the man, you unclean spirit!"

9 And He was asking him, "What is your name?" And he said to Him, "My name is Legion; for we are many."

10 And he began to implore Him earnestly not to send them out of the country.

11 Now there was a large herd of swine feeding nearby on the mountain.

12 The demons implored Him, saying, "Send us into the swine so that we may enter them."

13 Jesus gave them permission. And coming out, the unclean spirits entered the swine; and the herd rushed down the steep bank into the sea, about two thousand of them; and they were drowned in the sea.

• As you read this account, what gives you insight into Jesus' power and authority?

MARK 5:14–20

14 Their herdsmen ran away and reported it in the city and in the country. And the people came to see what it was that had happened.

15 They came to Jesus and observed the man who had been demon-possessed sitting down, clothed and in his right mind, the very man who

OBSERVE

Leader: Read Mark 5:14–20 aloud, slowly. Have the group…

• *mark all references to Jesus.*

• *draw a box around each mention of the man and mark it with a pitchfork. Switch to a box alone when the group decides it's time for the pitchfork to go.*

• *mark each reference to demon possession with a pitchfork.*

• *look back at the location you underlined in Mark 4:1, then double underline the location in Mark 5:20.*

Israel in the Time of Christ

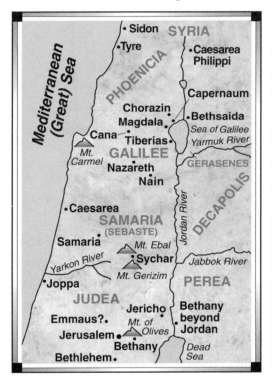

DISCUSS

• Look at the map to get a general idea of where these events were taking place. History tells us Gentiles were living in this area. (A Gentile is anyone who is not a Jew, a descendent of Abraham, Isaac, and Jacob.) This account confirms that the people were raising pigs, an animal

had had the "legion"; and they became frightened.

16 Those who had seen it described to them how it had happened to the demon-possessed man, and all about the swine.

17 And they began to implore Him to leave their region.

18 As He was getting into the boat, the man who had been demon-possessed was imploring Him that he might accompany Him.

19 And He did not let him, but He said to him, "Go home to your people and report to them what great things the Lord has done for you, and how He had mercy on you."

20 And he went away and began to proclaim in Decapolis what great things Jesus had done for him; and everyone was amazed.

considered unclean in the Jewish culture. So does this story tell you anything about Jesus and Gentiles?

• Contrast the attitude shown by the people of the area toward Jesus with that of the man who had been possessed.

• What insight does this incident give you into the people? What was their primary concern, as revealed by their response to Jesus and the liberation of this man?

MARK 5:21–34

21 When Jesus had crossed over again in the boat to the other side, a large crowd gathered around Him; and so He stayed by the seashore.

22 One of the synagogue officials named Jairus came up, and

OBSERVE

Jesus' reputation as a healer was spreading.

Leader: Read Mark 5:21–34 aloud. Have the group...
  • *mark each reference to **Jesus** as they have been doing.*
  • *place a big **J** over every reference to **Jairus**.*
  • *place a big **W** over every reference to **the woman**.*

DISCUSS

• Who was this man Jairus, and what did he believe about Jesus?

• Who was the woman? What did she believe about Jesus?

on seeing Him, fell at His feet

23 and implored Him earnestly, saying, "My little daughter is at the point of death; please come and lay Your hands on her, so that she will get well and live."

24 And He went off with him; and a large crowd was following Him and pressing in on Him.

25 A woman who had had a hemorrhage for twelve years,

26 and had endured much at the hands of many physicians, and had spent all that she had and was not helped at all, but rather had grown worse—

27 after hearing about Jesus, she came up in the crowd behind Him and touched His cloak.

28 For she thought, "If I just touch His garments, I will get well."

29 Immediately the flow of her blood was dried up; and she felt in her body that she was healed of her affliction.

30 Immediately Jesus, perceiving in Himself that the power proceeding from Him had gone forth, turned around in the crowd and said, "Who touched My garments?"

31 And His disciples said to Him, "You see

• What did Jairus and the woman have in common?

• What does verse 30 tell you about Jesus?

• What made the woman well, according to Jesus?

INSIGHT

Hebrews 11:6 tells us, "Without *faith* it is impossible to please [God], for he who comes to God must *believe* that He is and that He is a rewarder of those who seek Him."

The Greek word for "believe" is *pisteuo,* and the Greek word for "faith" is *pistis.* According to the Greek, *believe* is a verb, and *faith* is a noun. Believing, then, is far more than knowledge; it means you trust the knowledge you have and behave accordingly.

the crowd pressing in on You, and You say, 'Who touched Me?' "

³² And He looked around to see the woman who had done this.

³³ But the woman fearing and trembling, aware of what had happened to her, came and fell down before Him and told Him the whole truth.

³⁴ And He said to her, "Daughter, your faith has made you well; go in peace and be healed of your affliction."

MARK 5:35–43

35 While He was still speaking, they came from the house of the synagogue official, saying, "Your daughter has died; why trouble the Teacher anymore?"

36 But Jesus, overhearing what was being spoken, said to the synagogue official, "Do not be afraid any longer, only believe."

37 And He allowed no one to accompany Him, except Peter and James and John the brother of James.

38 They came to the house of the synagogue official; and He saw a commotion, and people loudly weeping and wailing.

OBSERVE

Let's read on to learn the answer to Jairus's plea for his daughter's life.

Leader: Read Mark 5:35–43 aloud. Have the group…
- *mark every reference to **Jesus**, including pronouns and synonyms such as **Teacher**.*
- *place a big **J** over every reference to **Jairus,** the synagogue official.*
- *mark any reference to **death** or **dying** with a tombstone symbol, like this:* ⌂

DISCUSS

• What was Jesus' exhortation to Jairus in verse 36?

• How does that compare with Jesus' words to the woman with the hemorrhage?

• Mark lets us know that the people laughed. What does their response tell you about their opinion of Jesus and what He said? Have you ever experienced a similar response when you've shared something from the Word of God?

• Who witnessed the raising of Jairus's daughter? Who was shut out? Do you have any idea why?

39 And entering in, He said to them, "Why make a commotion and weep? The child has not died, but is asleep."

40 They began laughing at Him. But putting them all out, He took along the child's father and mother and His own companions, and entered the room where the child was.

41 Taking the child by the hand, He said to her, "Talitha kum!" (which translated means, "Little girl, I say to you, get up!").

42 Immediately the girl got up and began to walk, for she was twelve years old. And immediately they were completely astounded.

43 And He gave them strict orders that no one should know about this, and He said that something should be given her to eat.

• How does Jesus regard people in pain? How would you describe His priorities, especially in comparison to those held by the society around Him?

• What have you learned this week about the touch of Jesus? Who, in this chapter received His touch and why?

• How can what you've observed make a difference in your life today?

WRAP IT UP

This chapter again declares and demonstrates who Jesus truly is, the Son of the Most High God. This proclamation initially came from a legion of demons possessing a man, who, once Jesus delivered him, became a proclaimer of Jesus and His mission. Then, freed from torment of Satan's demonic control, the man returned to his Gentile village with a message of mercy.

Mercy is the platform where we see the deity of Jesus. A trembling, bleeding woman is healed from an ailment that had consumed her life for twelve years, simply by the touch of Jesus. A young girl is raised from the dead as He takes her hand and simply says, "Get up, little girl."

And it happened because needy human beings sought Jesus, and He had compassion on them and healed them.

Oh, why would we run to another human being before we first sought His help, His guidance? He is the Son of the Most High God, who gives us life!

The question for us to consider is this: If Jesus is capable of doing these kind acts of mercy, what can He do for me? If He is the Son of the Most High God, what difference should that make in my personal journey with Jesus?

People love the miracles of Jesus. They cry for His touch in their time of need—but do they want to hear the words, the teaching of Jesus of Nazareth?

To the hometown folk of Nazareth, Jesus was no one special, just the son of a carpenter who lived in their unremarkable village with His mother, Mary, and His brothers and sisters and attended the only synagogue in town.

Mark 6, our final chapter in this portion of our study of Mark, begins as Jesus left the Sea of Galilee and returned to Nazareth, where He would encounter people who thought they knew Him well.

As we dig into the content of Mark 6, we need to ask: What's the purpose of the varied incidents recorded in this chapter? Why would God preserve them in His Word for the generations to come? How can they be of value to our lives today?

Let's see for ourselves…

OBSERVE

Leader: *Read Mark 6:1–6 aloud. Have the group…*

- *mark each reference to **Jesus** as they've done before.*
- *draw an open book over references to **teaching**, like this:* 📖
- *put an ear over **listeners**:* 👂

MARK 6:1–6

1 Jesus went out from there and came into His hometown; and His disciples followed Him.

2 When the Sabbath came, He began to teach in the synagogue; and the many

listeners were aston-
ished, saying, "Where
did this man get these
things, and what is
this wisdom given to
Him, and such mira-
cles as these performed
by His hands?

3 "Is not this the
carpenter, the son of
Mary, and brother of
James and Joses and
Judas and Simon? Are
not His sisters here
with us?" And they
took offense at Him.

4 Jesus said to them,
"A prophet is not
without honor except
in his hometown and
among his own rela-
tives and in his own
household."

5 And He could do
no miracle there except

DISCUSS

• What insight do you gain about Jesus
from the words of His listeners?

• What do you learn from marking references to teaching? What conclusions
can you draw regarding the reception it
received?

• How did Jesus describe Himself, and
what do we learn about His time in
Nazareth?

• What restrained Jesus from doing any
major works of power in His hometown
of Nazareth? How does this compare with
what we saw last week regarding Jairus
and the bleeding woman in Mark 5?

• In what ways do you see people today taking offense at Jesus?

OBSERVE

Leader: Read Mark 6:7–13 aloud. Have the group do the following:
- *Mark every reference to **Jesus.***
- *Draw an arrow under all references to **the Twelve.***
- *Mark the word **listen** with an ear.*
- *Mark references to **preaching** as you marked* teaching, *with an open book.*
- *Mark the word **repent** like this: ⤷*
- *Put a pitchfork over **unclean spirits.***

DISCUSS

• Look at the word *began* in verse 7. What happened with the Twelve that was different from their relationship to Jesus up to this point?

that He laid His hands on a few sick people and healed them.

6 And He wondered at their unbelief. And He was going around the villages teaching.

MARK 6:7–13

7 And He summoned the twelve and began to send them out in pairs, and gave them authority over the unclean spirits;

8 and He instructed them that they should take nothing for their journey, except a mere staff—no bread, no bag, no money in their belt—

9 but to wear sandals; and He added, "Do not put on two tunics."

10 And He said to them, "Wherever you enter a house, stay there until you leave town.

11 "Any place that does not receive you or listen to you, as you go out from there, shake the dust off the soles of your feet for a testimony against them."

12 They went out and preached that men should repent.

13 And they were casting out many demons and were anointing with oil many sick people and healing them.

• What do you learn from Jesus' instructions in verses 8–11?

• What was their message to be, and what do you think that means? Compare that with Mark 1:4, 14–15 in Week 1. See pages 5 and 8.

• What bore witness to the validity of their message?

• How does their assignment compare with what you've observed Jesus doing so far in the gospel of Mark?

• Look at where you marked the reference to preaching. Who is preaching? Where? How important do you think preaching is and why?

OBSERVE

Our last information on John the Baptist was that he had been taken into custody. Now we are going to learn what happened after that.

Leader: Read Mark 6:14–29 aloud, slowly. There are a lot of verses, but they detail a fast-paced story. Have the group...

- *mark every reference to **Jesus.***
- *draw a box over every reference to **Herod**, including pronouns and synonyms such as **the king.***
- *draw a squiggly line under each mention of **John the Baptist** as you did in Mark 1.*

DISCUSS

- Who did people, including Herod, think Jesus was? What does this tell you about their belief in respect to life after death?

Mark 6:14–29

14 And King Herod heard of it, for His name had become well known; and people were saying, "John the Baptist has risen from the dead, and that is why these miraculous powers are at work in Him."

15 But others were saying, "He is Elijah." And others were saying, "He is a prophet, like one of the prophets of old."

16 But when Herod heard of it, he kept saying, "John, whom I beheaded, has risen!"

17 For Herod himself had sent and had John arrested and bound in prison on account of Herodias, the wife of

his brother Philip, because he had married her.

18 For John had been saying to Herod, "It is not lawful for you to have your brother's wife."

19 Herodias had a grudge against him and wanted to put him to death and could not do so;

20 for Herod was afraid of John, knowing that he was a righteous and holy man, and he kept him safe. And when he heard him, he was very perplexed; but he used to enjoy listening to him.

21 A strategic day came when Herod on his birthday gave a banquet for his lords

• What kind of a witness was John to Herod, and how did Herod feel about John the Baptist?

• In a few words, why did Herod kill John? Just from reading the text, how do you think Herod felt about it?

• What lessons can you learn from John's beheading?

and military commanders and the leading men of Galilee;

22 and when the daughter of Herodias herself came in and danced, she pleased Herod and his dinner guests; and the king said to the girl, "Ask me for whatever you want and I will give it to you."

23 And he swore to her, "Whatever you ask of me, I will give it to you; up to half of my kingdom."

24 And she went out and said to her mother, "What shall I ask for?" And she said, "The head of John the Baptist."

25 Immediately she came in a hurry to the king and asked, saying,

"I want you to give me at once the head of John the Baptist on a platter."

26 And although the king was very sorry, yet because of his oaths and because of his dinner guests, he was unwilling to refuse her.

27 Immediately the king sent an executioner and commanded him to bring back his head. And he went and had him beheaded in the prison,

28 and brought his head on a platter, and gave it to the girl; and the girl gave it to her mother.

29 When his disciples heard about this, they came and took away his body and laid it in a tomb.

• Mark is a short gospel, yet the writer gives a lot of detail on John's death. Some believe Mark was motivated to write because of concern about the increasing persecution under Nero. If that is true, how might learning about the events detailed in these verses help his readers? And how might it help believers living in today's culture?

OBSERVE

We are about to observe another long passage that's best understood by looking at it as a whole—so get ready!

Leader: Read Mark 6:30–44 aloud. This time have the group...

- *mark each reference to **Jesus**.*
- *draw an arrow under the words **apostles** and **disciples**.*
- *draw an open book over each occurrence of **teach** and **taught**.*

INSIGHT

Apostle, or *apostello* in the Greek, means "one sent forth from another with a message." The only time the word *apostles* is used in the gospel of Mark is here in verse 30.

DISCUSS

- Read verse 30. How can you tell from the content of Mark 6 who the apostles are?

MARK 6:30–44

30 The apostles gathered together with Jesus; and they reported to Him all that they had done and taught.

31 And He said to them, "Come away by yourselves to a secluded place and rest a while." (For there were many people coming and going, and they did not even have time to eat.)

32 They went away in the boat to a secluded place by themselves.

33 The people saw them going, and many recognized them and ran there together on foot from all the cities, and got there ahead of them.

34 When Jesus went ashore, He saw a large crowd, and He felt compassion for them because they were like sheep without a shepherd; and He began to teach them many things.

35 When it was already quite late, His disciples came to Him and said, "This place is desolate and it is already quite late;

36 send them away so that they may go into the surrounding countryside and villages and buy themselves something to eat."

37 But He answered them, "You give them something to eat!" And they said to Him, "Shall we go and spend

• Where did Jesus take the apostles and for what purpose? And what could they learn from the Master?

• What was Jesus' assessment of the crowd in verse 34 and what did He do? Do you get any idea from the text how long He did it?

• Shepherds were to feed their flocks. So what do you learn from verses 34 and 35 about Jesus and what He did out of His concern?

• You marked the references to teaching (preaching) in verses 2, 6, 12, 30, and 34. Review each again; what do these verses tell you about teaching? Consider the five Ws and an H: who, what, when, where, why, and how.

• What lessons, if any, can be learned from these verses and applied to us today?

• Review the facts of the feeding of the multitude. What precipitated this event? How many were fed, with what, and how much was left over?

two hundred denarii on bread and give them something to eat?"

38 And He said to them, "How many loaves do you have? Go look!" And when they found out, they said, "Five, and two fish."

39 And He commanded them all to sit down by groups on the green grass.

40 They sat down in groups of hundreds and of fifties.

41 And He took the five loaves and the two fish, and looking up toward heaven, He blessed the food and broke the loaves and He kept giving them to the disciples to set before them; and He divided up the two fish among them all.

42 They all ate and were satisfied,

43 and they picked up twelve full baskets of the broken pieces, and also of the fish.

44 There were five thousand men who ate the loaves.

MARK 6:45–52

45 Immediately Jesus made His disciples get into the boat and go ahead of Him to the other side to Bethsaida, while He Himself was sending the crowd away.

46 After bidding them farewell, He left

• Who would know these facts in the greatest detail? So who took part in the feeding of the multitude?

• What would this event show the disciples about Jesus?

OBSERVE

Keeping that last question in mind, let's see what happened immediately after the feeding of the multitude.

Leader: Read Mark 6:45–52 aloud. Have the group do the following:
- *Mark each reference to **Jesus**.*
- *Draw an arrow under every mention of **the disciples**.*
- *Double underline references to **location**.*
- *Circle all references to **time**.*

DISCUSS

• As you look at where you marked the references to Jesus, what do you learn about Him and His relationship with His Father? With His disciples?

• Jesus told His disciples to take courage and not be afraid, because He was the one walking toward them. What had they just seen Him do? And what had they seen Him do before that in another storm?

• What do you learn from verses 51 and 52 about the disciples, the Twelve? Why were they astonished? What does that tell you about them?

• How could you apply Jesus' words to the Twelve in verse 50 to your life?

for the mountain to pray.

47 When it was evening, the boat was in the middle of the sea, and He was alone on the land.

48 Seeing them straining at the oars, for the wind was against them, at about the fourth watch of the night He came to them, walking on the sea; and He intended to pass by them.

49 But when they saw Him walking on the sea, they supposed that it was a ghost, and cried out;

50 for they all saw Him and were terrified. But immediately He spoke with them and said to them, "Take courage; it is I, do not be afraid."

51 Then He got into the boat with them, and the wind stopped; and they were utterly astonished,

52 for they had not gained any insight from the incident of the loaves, but their heart was hardened.

MARK 6:53–56

53 When they had crossed over they came to land at Gennesaret, and moored to the shore.

54 When they got out of the boat, immediately the people recognized Him,

• What insight(s) have you gained about Jesus over these past six weeks? If you are a true follower of Christ, how can this new knowledge give you courage in the midst of trials?

OBSERVE

Well done. We've come to the final verses of Mark 6. You are to be commended for your faithfulness.

Leader: Read Mark 6:53–56 aloud. Once again have the group...
  • *double underline anything that tells* __*where.*__
  • *mark every reference to **Jesus**.*

DISCUSS

• Where did Jesus go, and what happened in those places?

• We've learned much these past six weeks about touching Jesus—not just about those who touched Him, but about why they would want to touch Him. What is the most significant truth you've learned about Jesus? What area of your life most needs the touch of Jesus?

55 and ran about that whole country and began to carry here and there on their pallets those who were sick, to the place they heard He was.

56 Wherever He entered villages, or cities, or countryside, they were laying the sick in the market places, and imploring Him that they might just touch the fringe of His cloak; and as many as touched it were being cured.

WRAP IT UP

Are you straining against the winds of difficulty, adversity, temptation? Worn out from the battle? Do you feel in danger of being tossed overboard by the storm, capsizing, and never making it to the shore of peace and safety?

Oh, beloved, for whom Jesus died, don't harden your heart. Don't try to go it alone. Look for Jesus. He's there walking toward you on the turbulent water. Take courage. Remember all you've learned about Him just in these six chapters of Mark. He is the same yesterday, today, forever. If Jesus is the Son of the Most High God—and He is, as even the demons know—nothing and no one is beyond His control, authority, or ability. Call to Him, ask Him to get in the boat with you.

He will because He cares for you—as you will see for yourself through the next two 40-Minute Bible Studies on the gospel of Mark: *Jesus: Listening for His Voice* and *Jesus: Understanding His Death and Resurrection.* There is far more for you to learn about Jesus and from Him, truths you need to see for yourself about the life, ministry, and teaching of the One who came to lay down His life for you.

Surely you are not going to trust a Jesus you do not know. Shallow knowledge produces a shallow relationship! Make it a priority to finish studying the gospel of Mark, beloved, so that Jesus might naturally become your first resort when the winds of adversity blow.

ABOUT DAVID ARTHUR

DAVID ARTHUR serves as chief executive officer of Precept Ministries International. Having been mentored by his parents, Jack and Kay Arthur, in the value of inductive Bible study, he shares their passion for establishing people in God's Word.

Prior to his role at Precept, David worked in the business world with IBM and small businesses. Starting in 1999 David served for several years as a pastor in both the Presbyterian Church of America and the Associate Reformed Presbyterian Church. Just before coming to Precept, he was vice president with Generous Giving, working with givers and pastors. David is a gifted and passionate teacher of God's Word. He holds a bachelor's degree in organizational management from Covenant College and a master of arts in theological studies from Reformed Theological Seminary.

Contact Precept Ministries International for more information about inductive Bible studies in your area.

Precept Ministries International
PO Box 182218
Chattanooga, TN 37422-7218
800-763-8280
www.precept.org